To

From

Written and compiled by Lois Rock
Illustrations copyright © 2005 Helen Cann

This edition copyright © 2013 Lion Hudson

Published by Lion Children's Books
an imprint of
Lion Hudson plc
Wilkinson House, Jordan Hill Road,
Oxford OX2 8DR, England
www.lionhudson.com/lionchildrens

ISBN 978 0 7459 6403 4

First edition 2013

Acknowledgments
All unattributed prayers are by Lois Rock, copyright © Lion Hudson.
Bible extracts are taken or adapted from the Good News Bible published by the Bible
Societies and HarperCollins Publishers, © American Bible Society 1994, used with
permission.
The Lord's Prayer (on page 12) from *Common Worship: Services and Prayers for the
Church of England* (Church House Publishing, 2000) is copyright © The English
Language Liturgical Consultation, 1988 and is reproduced by permission of the
publishers.

A catalogue record for this book is available from the British Library

Printed and bound in China, April 2013, LH17

PRAYERS
from the
BIBLE

Written and compiled by Lois Rock
Illustrated by Helen Cann

LI N
CHILDREN'S

Jesus told his disciples to be faithful in prayer, saying:

"Ask, and you will receive;
seek, and you will find;
knock, and the door will be opened to you.

"For everyone who asks will receive,
and anyone who seeks will find,
and the door will be opened to those who knock.

"Your Father in heaven will give good things
to those who ask him."

From Matthew 7:7–8, 11

Contents

Prayer

O God,
I will pray to you in the morning,
I will pray to you at sunrise.

I will ask you to show me the way that I should go.

I will ask you to protect me from the people
who do not like me, who want to hurt me.

I will trust in you to protect me,
I will trust in your love.

From Psalm 5

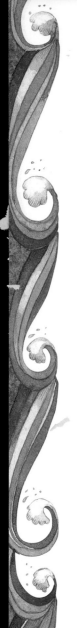

Do not worry

Do not worry,
but in prayer
ask God for what you need
with thankful heart
and simple trust
for God is Lord indeed.

Then peace
far wider than the sky
and deeper than the sea
will fill your heart
and soul and mind
now and eternally.

Based on Philippians 4:6–7

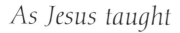

As Jesus taught

Our Father in heaven,
hallowed be your name,
your kingdom come,
your will be done,
on earth as in heaven.
Give us today our daily bread.
Forgive us our sins
as we forgive those who sin against us.
Lead us not into temptation
but deliver us from evil.

The Lord's Prayer,
from Matthew 6:9–13 and Luke 11:2–4

For the kingdom, the power,
and the glory are yours
now and for ever.
Amen

A traditional ending for the prayer

Praising God

I praise the Lord with all my soul,
my strength, my heart, my mind:
he blesses me with love and grace
and is for ever kind.

Based on Psalm 103:1–4

God's greatness

O God, your greatness is seen in all the world!

I look at the sky, which you have made;
at the moon and the stars, which you set in their
places, and I wonder:

Who am I, that you think of me?
What is humankind, that you care for us?
O God, your greatness is seen in all the world!

From Psalm 8:1, 3–4

God's love and care

Who would make a tiny flower
so beautiful? It lasts an hour!
The bloom then quickly fades away
before the setting of the day.

Who would make a tiny leaf
so intricate? Its life is brief:
a season in the summer sun
before its fluttering life is done.

The One who made both great and small,
who loves and cares for one and all
on land and water, sky and sea:
the One who loves and cares for me.

Based on Jesus' Sermon on the Mount, Matthew 6:25–34

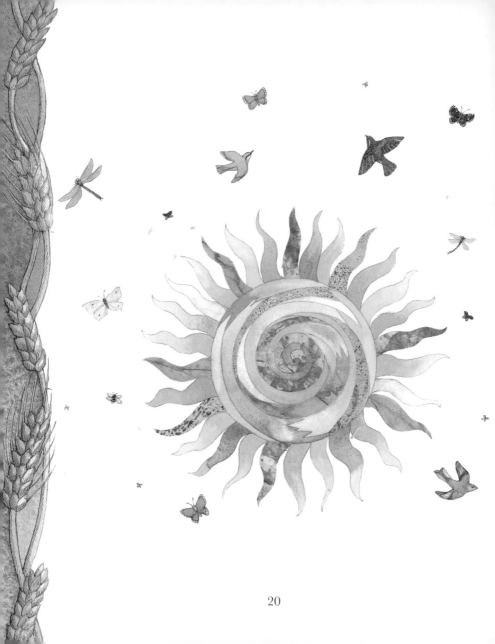

Harvest

Bless the Lord of heaven above
Sing to God with joy and love

Giving thanks for sun and rain
For the springtime once again

For the seeds that lay unseen
For their waking leaves of green

For the flowers that unfold
For the harvest, rich and gold

Bless the Lord of heaven above
Sing to God with joy and love.

Based on Psalm 65:8–13

Sing out loud

Sing to God with thankfulness,
sing a song of praise,
sing out loud and joyfully,
sing out all your days.

From Psalm 95

Praise the Lord with trumpets –
all praise to him belongs;
praise him with your music,
your dancing and your songs!

Based on Psalm 150

Forgiving and Forgiven

I told God everything:
I told God about all the wrong things I had done.
I gave up trying to pretend.
I gave up trying to hide.
I knew that the only thing to do was to confess.

And God forgave me.

Based on Psalm 32:5

Confessing

God, have mercy on me, a sinner!

From Jesus' parable of the Pharisee and the tax collector,
Luke 18:13

Come back to the Lord your God.
He is kind and full of mercy;
he is patient and keeps his promise;
he is always ready to forgive and not punish.

Joel 2:13

27

Forgiven

Take my wrongdoing
and throw it away,
down in the deep of the sea;
welcome me into your kingdom of love
for all of eternity.

Based on Micah 7:18–20

Jesus, guide your straying sheep
from the wild mountain steep
to where meadow grass grows deep
and the quiet waters sleep.

Based on Jesus' saying, "I am the Good Shepherd": John 10:7–16

Forgiving

Jesus said,
"Do not judge others, so that God will not judge you,
for God will judge you in the same way as you judge
others, and he will apply to you the same rules you
apply to others."

Matthew 7:1–2

Seven
times seven
I freely forgive
and seven
times seventy more.
Lord, give me the grace
to forgive
and forgive,
again
and again
I implore.

Based on Jesus' words to Peter, Matthew 18:22

Following the Way

I will choose the narrow path,
I will walk the straight,
Through the wide and winding world
Up to heaven's gate.

Based on Matthew 7:13–14

The Great Commandments

O Lord,

I have heard your laws.

May I worship you.

May I worship you alone.

May all I say and do show respect for your holy name.

May I honour the weekly day of rest.

May I show respect for my parents.

May I reject violence so that I never take a life.

May I learn to be loyal in friendship and so learn to
be faithful in marriage.

May I not steal what belongs to others.

May I not tell lies to destroy another person's
reputation.

May I not be envious of what others have, but may I
learn to be content with the good things you give me.

Based on the Ten Commandments, Exodus 20

Helping others

Dear God,
When I see someone in trouble,
may I know when to stop and help
and when to hurry to fetch help;
but may I never pass by,
pretending I did not see.

Based on Jesus' parable of the Good Samaritan,
Luke 10:25–37

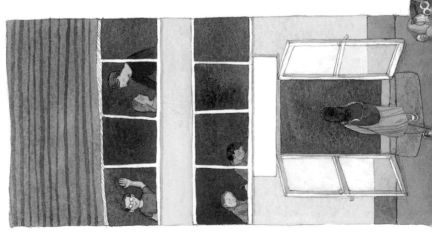

Dear God,

Help me to love other people so well that they
recognize me as one of your friends.

Based on John 13:34–35

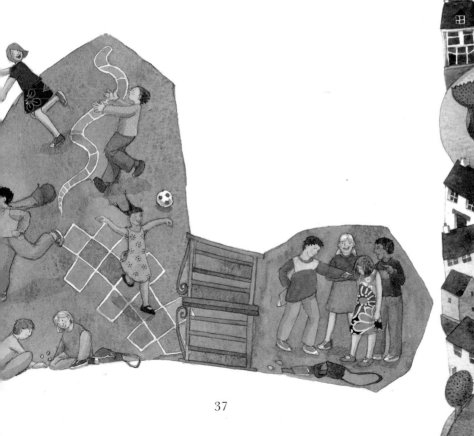

Seeing Jesus in others

Lord Jesus,
Make me as kind to others
as I would want to be to you.

Make me as generous to others
as I would want to be to you.

38

May I take time to help them
as I would want to take time to help you.

May I take trouble to help them
as I would want to take trouble to help you.

May I look into the faces of those I meet
and see your face.

Based on Matthew 25:37–40

Showing God's love

Help me, Lord, to show your love.

Help me to be patient and kind,
not jealous or conceited or proud.
May I never be ill-mannered, selfish
   or irritable;
may I be quick to forgive
   and forget.

May I not gloat over wrongdoing,
but rather be glad about things that are
good and true.

May I never give up loving:
may my faith and hope and patience never fail.

May I put my trust
in your eternal love.

Based on 1 Corinthians 13:4–7

41

For All the World

God says this:

Do not cling onto what happened in the past.

Watch for the new thing I am going to do.

I will make a path through the wilderness

and those who travel on it will be joyful again.

Based on the words of the prophet Isaiah 43:18–21

Let there be peace

O God,
Settle the quarrels among the nations.

May they hammer their swords into ploughs
and their spears into pruning knives.

Where the tanks now roll, let there be tractors;
where the landmines explode, let the fields grow crops.

Let there be a harvest of fruit and grain
and peace that all the world can share.

Based on Micah 4:3–5

God's love and goodness

Dear God,
When everything is going wrong I sometimes
wonder why you let bad things happen.

But then you open my eyes to the majesty of your
world, and I know once more that you are far greater
than I can imagine, and I believe once more that your
love and goodness will not be overcome.

Based on the book of Job

A new creation

O God,
We wait patiently for you to remake the world
as a place of joy and happiness;
where babies thrive,
where the elderly are strong;
where everyone has a home
and a fruitful garden;
where the world's creatures are at peace
with one another
and with all of humankind.

Based on Isaiah 65

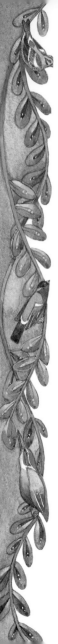

God's kingdom come

The kingdom of God
is like a tree
growing through all eternity.

In its branches, birds may nest;
in its shade we all may rest.

Based on Jesus' parable of the
mustard seed, Matthew 13

God's Blessing

May the Lord bless you,
may the Lord take care of you;
May the Lord be kind to you,
may the Lord be gracious to you;
May the Lord look on you with favour,
may the Lord give you peace.

From Numbers 6:24–26

Spirit of God

Spirit of God
put love in my life.

Spirit of God
put joy in my life.

Spirit of God
put peace in my life.

Spirit of God
make me patient.

Spirit of God
make me kind.

Spirit of God
make me good.

Spirit of God
give me faithfulness.

Spirit of God
give me humility.

Spirit of God
give me self-control.

From Galatians 5:22–23

Through the darkness

I sing a song of praise to God
throughout the darkest night,
for guarding me, for guiding me
to know what's good and right.
No evil things will frighten me,
no shadows from the tomb,
for God is light and life and power
to scatter midnight's gloom.

Based on Psalm 16:7–11

The Lord is my light and my salvation;
I will fear no one.
The Lord protects me from all danger;
I will never be afraid.

Psalm 27:1

My Shepherd God

Dear God, you are my shepherd,
You give me all I need,
    You take me where the grass grows
      green
      And I can safely feed.

    You take me where the water
    Is quiet and cool and clear;
    And there I rest and know I'm safe
For you are always near.

Based on Psalm 23

A night-time prayer

When I lie down,
I go to sleep in peace;
you alone, O Lord,
keep me perfectly safe.

Psalm 4:8

Index of First Lines